Colin Powell

By Wil Mara

Consultant
Jeanne Clidas, Ph.D.
National Reading Consultant
and
Professor of Reading, SUNY Brockport

Children's Press ®
A Division of Scholastic Inc.
New York   Toronto   London   Auckland   Sydney
Mexico City   New Delhi   Hong Kong
Danbury, Connecticut

Designer: Herman Adler Design
Photo Researcher: Caroline Anderson
The photo on the cover shows Colin Powell.

Library of Congress Cataloging-in-Publication Data

Mara, Wil.
  Colin Powell / by Wil Mara.
    p. cm. – (Rookie biography)
Includes index.
Summary: Presents a brief overview of the life of the first African
American Secretary of State.
  ISBN 0-516-25877-X (lib. bdg.)   0-516-27918-1 (pbk.)
  1. Powell, Colin L.–Juvenile literature. 2. Statesmen–United
States–Biography–Juvenile literature. 3. African American
generals–Biography–Juvenile literature. 4. Generals–United
States–Biography–Juvenile literature. 5. United States.
Army–Biography–Juvenile literature. [1. Powell, Colin L.
2. Cabinet officers. 3. Generals. 4. African Americans—Biography.]
I. Title. II. Series.
  E840.8.P64M37 2003
  973.931'092–dc21

                                    2003004428

CHILDREN'S PRESS, and ROOKIE BIOGRAPHIES™, and associated
logos are trademarks and or registered trademarks of Scholastic Library
Publishing. SCHOLASTIC and associated logos are trademarks and or
registered trademarks of Scholastic Inc.
1 2 3 4 5 6 7 8 9 10 R 12 11 10 09 08 07 06 05 04 03

Colin Powell has never
been afraid of hard work.

He was born on April 5, 1937,
in Harlem, New York.

Harlem, New York

Powell did not like school when he was a young boy. He liked to play with his friends instead.

Colin's parents wanted him and his sister to go to college. They taught their children that hard work was important.

Powell started going to the City College of New York in 1954.

He saw students wearing uniforms (YOO-nuh-formz) there. They were in the military (MIL-uh-ter-ee).

The military is a group of people who will fight to protect a country.

The army and the navy are part of the United States military.

Army

14

Powell loved the idea of being in the military. He joined the army when he was 17. The army helped him pay for college.

After college, Powell was
in the army every day.

People quickly saw that he was a good leader. He was fair and honest with his soldiers (SOLE-jurs).

Powell got many promotions (pruh-MOH-shuhns). Promotion means to give someone a more important job.

Later, Powell became a general.

19

In 1987, Powell was asked to work for the President of the United States.

The president wanted to hear his ideas on how to run the military.

Two years later, Powell was
put in charge of the United
States military.

He was the first African American
to ever have that job.

General Powell left the military in 1993. He wanted to spend more time with his family.

He wrote a book about his life.

In 2001, Powell was asked to be America's Secretary (SEK-ruh-ter-ee) of State. This was also a job no African American had ever had.

Colin Powell shows us that you can go far in life if you work hard.

He is an American hero.

Words You Know

Colin Powell

general

Harlem

leader

30

military

Secretary of State

uniform

31

Index

About the Author

More than fifty published books bear Wil Mara's name. He has written both fiction and nonfiction, for both children and adults. He lives with his family in northern New Jersey.

Photo Credits